TABLE OF CONTENTS

Synopsis 1

Pre-Reading Activities 2

Word Web 3

Chapters I - III .... 4 - 6

Chapters IV - VIII .... 7 - 8

Chapters IX, X .... 9 - 10

Chapters XI - XIV .... 11 - 12

Chapter XV - XVIII .... 13 - 14

Chapters XIX - XXII .... 15 - 16

Cloze Activity 17

Post-Reading Activities .... 18 - 19

Suggestions For Further Reading 20

Answer Key .... 21 - 22

Novel-Ties® are printed on recycled paper.

The purchase of this study guide entitles an individual teacher to reproduce pages for use in a classroom. Reproduction for use in an entire school or school system or for commercial use is prohibited. Beyond the classroom use by an individual teacher, reproduction, transmittal or retrieval of this work is prohibited without written permission from the publisher.

Copyright © 1983, 2003, 2014 by LEARNING LINKS

For the Teacher

This reproducible study guide to use in conjunction with the book *Charlotte's Web* consists of lessons for guided reading. Written in chapter-by-chapter format, the guide contains a synopsis, pre-reading activities, vocabulary and comprehension exercises, as well as extension activities to be used as follow-up to the novel.

In a homogeneous classroom, whole class instruction with one title is appropriate. In a heterogeneous classroom, reading groups should be formed: each group works on a different novel at its reading level. Depending upon the length of time devoted to reading in the classroom, each novel, with its guide and accompanying lessons, may be completed in three to six weeks.

Begin using NOVEL-TIES for guided reading by distributing the novel and a folder to each child. Distribute duplicated pages of the study guide for students to place in their folders. After examining the cover and glancing through the book, students can participate in several pre-reading activities. Vocabulary questions should be considered prior to reading a chapter or group of chapters; all other work should be done after the chapter has been read. Comprehension questions can be answered orally or in writing. The classroom teacher should determine the amount of work to be assigned, always keeping in mind that readers must be nurtured and that the ultimate goal is encouraging students' love of reading.

The benefits of using NOVEL-TIES are numerous. Students read good literature in the original, rather than in abridged or edited form. The good reading habits will be transferred to the books students read independently. Passive readers become active, avid readers.

SYNOPSIS

Charlotte's Web is a touching story about love, loneliness, loyalty, and friendship. The world of this book is seen mainly through the eyes of Wilbur, an endearing pig, and his erudite friend Charlotte, a spider. They are both creatures with human emotions with which readers of all ages can empathize.

Wilbur begins life as the runt of a litter on the Arable family's farm. Even though young Fern Arable makes a household pet of him, Wilbur must eventually move to Zuckerman's farm and take up the life of a barnyard animal. Just when life seems gloomiest, Wilbur is befriended by Charlotte, the spider who lives in the Zuckerman barn.

Charlotte devotes her life to changing Wilbur's image, thereby saving him from inevitable slaughter at Christmas. Relying on the power of suggestion to accomplish her goal, she writes complimentary words about Wilbur in her web. People are so astounded with this miracle that they begin to believe that Wilbur is indeed a special pig. Catering to the gluttonous interests of Templeton the rat, Charlotte bribes him into finding scraps of newsprint that might contain additional appropriate words for her web.

When it is time for the country fair, Zuckerman enters Wilbur into competition. Even an ailing Charlotte trails along in order to observe her friend's moment of triumph. Wilbur, buttermilk-washed and radiant, becomes a prime attraction at the fair and is awarded a special bronze medal. Just when Wilbur's fate seems secure, however, Charlotte lays her eggs and goes into a rapid physical decline. Wilbur, distraught over Charlotte, decides to bring the precious egg sac containing her babies back to the farm, while Charlotte, unable to travel, must die alone at the fairgrounds. Although Wilbur has the friendship and company of Charlotte's progeny for the rest of his long life, he never forgets Charlotte, the true friend who rescued him from loneliness and an untimely death.

PRE-READING ACTIVITIES

1. Preview the book by reading the title and the author's name and by looking at the illustration on the cover. What do you think this book will be about? Have you read any other books by the same author?

2. The story of *Charlotte's Web* takes place on a farm. Have you ever visited a farm, or do you live on a farm? What is the difference between the way animals are usually treated on a farm and in a town? Why do people have pets? Why do they keep livestock? Do farmers ever make their livestock into pets?

3. Display some pictures of a farm on a class bulletin board. Show a barn, barnyard animals, crops growing in a field, etc. If possible, also find and display pictures of a rural country fair. What do people do at a country fair? What kinds of prizes are awarded?

4. Look at the copyright page opposite the contents page at the beginning of the book. Notice that this book was originally granted a copyright in 1952. Why might a book remain popular after so many years?

5. **Science Connection:** Do some research to learn about the life cycle of spiders. Find answers to the following questions:
    - What is their usual habitat?
    - What do they eat?
    - How do they reproduce?
    - What is their typical life cycle?

6. **Cooperative Learning Activity:** Have you ever read any books or seen any films in which animals are able to talk and act like humans? If so, what books and films were they? Work with a small group of your classmates to compile a list of these books and films. Then discuss why you think the authors gave human characteristics to animals.

7. You and your classmates may consult the *Guiness Book of World Records* to find amazing facts about plants and animals. Make a list of record-breaking animals. Compare your own list with those of your classmates.

8. Make two copies of the word web on the following page. Before you read the book, follow the directions to complete one copy. Complete the second copy after you finish Chapter Five.

WORD WEB

Directions:

- Before you read the book – On the lines surrounding the name of each animal, write descriptive words that you associate with each creature.

- After reading Chapter Five – On the lines surrounding the name of each animal, write the descriptive words that the author uses to describe Wilbur, Templeton, and Charlotte.

- Compare your words on the first copy of the web to the author's words on the second copy. How is the author trying to shape your opinion of each animal?

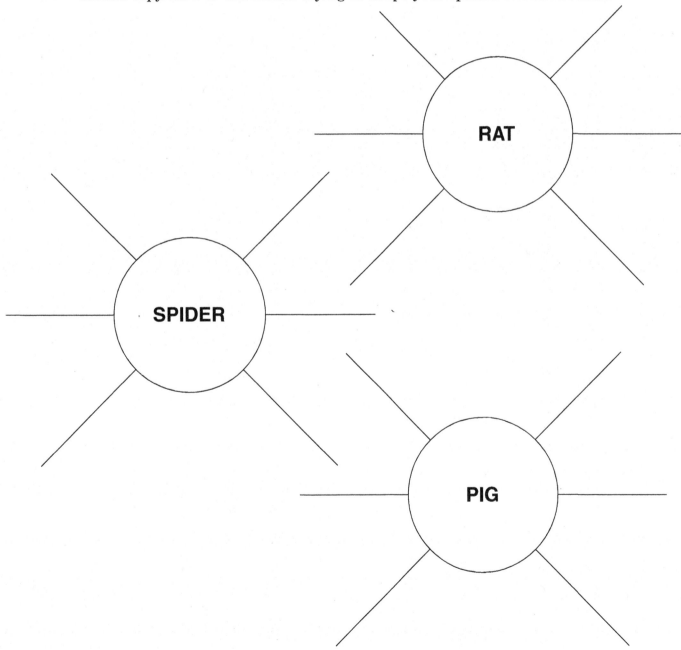

CHAPTERS I – III

Vocabulary: Use the context to figure out the meaning of the underlined word in each of the following sentences. Compare your definition with a dictionary definition.

1. All of the farmers agreed that the small, weak runt would never amount to anything.

   Your definition: _____

   Dictionary definition: _____

2. Having become fond of the pig, the little boy thought it would be a terrible case of injustice to kill a pig just because it was small.

   Your definition: _____

   Dictionary definition: _____

3. Such a fine specimen of a pig would bring in a lot of money at the farm auction.

   Your definition: _____

   Dictionary definition: _____

4. The little girl was in a blissful mood as she looked out at the beautiful day, waiting for her best friend to come and play.

   Your definition: _____

   Dictionary definition: _____

5. A pig will use its snout to root out food in the dirt.

   Your definition: _____

   Dictionary definition: _____

6. The falling star traveled so fast that it seemed to vanish shortly after it appeared.

   Your definition: _____

   Dictionary definition: _____

7. After running for an hour in the sun, the athlete was soaked with perspiration.

   Your definition: _____

   Dictionary definition: _____

8. There was so much commotion in the cafeteria that no one heard the announcements.

   Your definition: _____

   Dictionary definition: _____

Chapters I – III (cont.)

> Read to find out why Mr. Arable doesn't want a pet pig on his farm.

Questions:

1. Why did Mr. Arable want to kill the baby pig?
2. Why did Fern object to the killing?
3. Why did Mr. Arable change his mind?
4. When Wilbur was a baby, why did Fern say, "Every day was a happy day, and every night was peaceful"?
5. How did Fern's father bring her great happiness to a sudden end? Why did her father feel this way?
6. How did Wilbur's new home compare to his old home?
7. What was the first hint that the animals on the farm were communicating with each other?
8. Why did Wilbur run away from Zuckerman's farm? Why did he return to the farm?

Questions for Discussion:

1. What problems could arise from raising a barnyard animal as a pet?
2. What do you think Mr. Zuckerman meant when he said, "Yes, he'll make a good pig"?

Word Study:

I. Use a dictionary to look up the word "arable." Why did the author name Fern's parents Mr. and Mrs. Arable?

_____

_____

Why do you think the girl is called "Fern"?

_____

_____

II. Draw a line from each animal on the left to the word which names its offspring on the right.

1. pig   a. gosling
2. cow   b. puppy
3. goat   c. foal
4. horse   d. piglet
5. goose   e. kid
6. dog   f. calf

Chapters I – III (cont.)

Literary Device: Hook

A hook in literature refers to the opening of a story that grabs the reader's attention. Reread the beginning of *Charlotte's Web* to notice the hook. Why do you think the author chose this beginning?

_____

_____

What does this beginning suggest about the rest of the book?

_____

_____

Writing Activity:

Write about a time when you thought you might lose something or someone you loved. Describe the object of your affection and tell why it was dear to you. What was the outcome of your dilemma?

CHAPTERS IV – VIII

Vocabulary: Draw a line from each word on the left to its meaning on the right. Then use the numbered words to fill in the blanks in the sentences below.

1. anesthetic
2. rigid
3. conspiracy
4. appalled
5. lair
6. innocent
7. morsel
8. crafty

a. evil plan
b. tricky; sly
c. overcome with horror
d. faultless; unsophisticated
e. hideaway of a wild animal
f. small portion
g. stiff; unbending
h. substance that causes someone to lose physical feeling

. . . .

1. The dentist gave me a(n) _____ before she began drilling my tooth.
2. I was so hungry I ate every _____ of food on my plate.
3. A(n) _____ steel beam supports the building.
4. The child had such a(n) _____ look on his face that it was hard to believe he ate all the cookies.
5. We were _____ by the reports of the poor conditions of the factory workers.
6. The _____ fox figured out a way to get into the chicken coop.
7. The wolf brought food back to its _____.
8. The _____ to rob the bank was foiled by a tip to the police ahead of time.

> Read to find out about Wilbur's new friend at the farm.

Questions:

1. Why did Wilbur become depressed at Mr. Zuckerman's farm?
2. How did the animals react to Wilbur's sadness?
3. How did Charlotte explain her web-spinning and hunting behavior?

Chapters IV – VIII (cont.)

4. What did the goose mean when she said that Wilbur "is really a very innocent little pig"?

5. On the day when the goslings were born, how did Templeton's presence remind the reader of nature's ugly side?

6. How did Wilbur react to the bad news that the old sheep told him? How did Charlotte react to this news?

7. What did Mrs. Arable think when Fern told her that the animals talked to each other? What did Mr. Arable think?

Questions for Discussion:

1. Why do you think the author repeated the word "rain" so many times at the beginning of Chapter IV?

2. What was Charlotte's first word to Wilbur on the day they met? Why do you think the author chose this word for her opening statement? Why didn't she just say "hello"?

3. Return to the Word Web that you began in the Pre-Reading Activities on page three of this study guide. Fill in the second Word Web. Has the author changed your feelings about each of these animals?

Science Connection:

Do some research on rats to learn about their habits, what they eat, and where they live. How much of the material written about Templeton is based on facts about rats and how much is fiction?

Writing Activity:

Tell how Charlotte's statement that friendship is a gamble relates to your own life. Write about a time when you or someone you know was afraid to befriend someone, or an established friend revealed surprising things.

CHAPTERS IX, X

Vocabulary: Antonyms are words with opposite meanings. Draw a line from each word in column A to its antonym in column B. Then use the words in column A to fill in the blanks in the sentences below.

A	B
1. sedentary	a. skeptical
2. vague	b. ascend
3. gullible	c. proud
4. boastful	d. humble
5. descend	e. dawn
6. embarrassed	f. active
7. twilight	g. praise
8. complain	h. clear

. . . .

1. I was _____ when I slipped and fell walking across the stage.
2. People who lead _____ lives must exercise to stay healthy.
3. Be careful as you _____ the narrow, twisted staircase.
4. If you _____ to the manager of the restaurant, she will turn down the air conditioner.
5. It is difficult to drive at _____ because shapes and distances are hard to see.
6. Children are warned not to be _____ when strangers offer them sweets.
7. The driving directions were so _____ that I got lost on the way to your house.
8. If you are _____ about your new bicycle, you will upset your friend who has one that is old and rusty.

> Read to learn about Charlotte's special talent.

Questions:

1. How did Wilbur's innocence lead him to try an impossible task?
2. What was Charlotte's opinion of humans' web-spinning ability?
3. Why did Charlotte prefer her own kind of life to that of human society?

Chapters IX, X (cont.)

4. Why did Charlotte like the environment of Wilbur's pen?
5. Compare and contrast the way Avery and Fern treated animals.
6. How did a rotten goose egg save Charlotte and her web?

Questions for Discussion:

1. In what ways did Charlotte seem like a mother to Wilbur as well as a friend?
2. How do you think Charlotte plans to save Wilbur's life?

Literary Device: Cliffhanger

A cliffhanger in literature is a device borrowed from silent, serialized films in which a chapter or episode ended at a moment of great tension or suspense. In a book, it usually appears at the end of a chapter to encourage the reader to continue reading. What is the cliffhanger at the end of Chapter X?

_____

_____

Social Studies Connection:

Do some research to learn about what is now named the Ed Koch Queensborough Bridge or the 59th Street Bridge in New York City. Find out when it was built, how long it took to build, what land masses it connects, and why it is important to New York City's transportation system. Then find a picture of the bridge to learn why Charlotte compared it to her web.

Writing Activity:

Pretend that two of your real or imaginary pets could talk. Write a dialogue between them expressing a problem they have and a possible solution.

CHAPTERS XI – XIV

Vocabulary: Use the context to figure out the meaning of the underlined word in each of the following sentences. Then use a dictionary to check your answers. Record your responses on the chart below.

- All the animals seemed completely <u>bewildered</u> as they tried to figure out how to make a web.
- Wilbur was so worried about his future that he <u>neglected</u> to eat.
- Templeton's <u>destiny</u> was linked to Wilbur's as he depended on eating Wilbur's leftovers.
- It seemed to the barnyard animals that people were <u>incessant</u> talkers.
- After a day of field work, Mr. Zuckerman felt tired from his day's <u>exertions</u>.
- When making a web, Charlotte would first create the <u>radial</u> lines for support, and then connect them with the <u>orb</u> lines.
- With a <u>solemn</u> expression on his face, Wilbur begged Charlotte for help.
- After climbing under the barbed wire fence, his clothing became <u>tattered</u>.

Word	Your Definition	Dictionary Definition
1. bewildered		
2. neglected		
3. destiny		
4. incessant		
5. exertions		
6. radial		
7. orb		
8. solemn		
9. tattered		

Read to find out how a spider can improve the image of a pig.

Chapters XI – XIV (cont.)

Questions:

1. Why did Charlotte write "Some Pig" in her web? What effect did this message have upon Mr. Zuckerman, Mrs. Zuckerman, Lurvy, and the Minister?
2. Why was Chapter XI called "The Miracle"? What did the Minister and Mr. Zuckerman mean when they suggested that the writing in the web could be a sign?
3. How did the animals convince Templeton to cooperate with them in order to save Wilbur's life?
4. How did Charlotte's message change the Zuckermans' attitude toward their pig and Wilbur's own attitude about himself?
5. How did Dr. Dorian convince Mrs. Arable not to worry about Fern?

Questions for Discussion:

1. How did the power of suggestion influence the Zuckermans' feelings about their pig?
2. Can you recall a time when compliments made you feel better about yourself?
3. What was the implied moral in each of the stories Charlotte told Wilbur about her spider cousins?

Word Study:

On the lines of this word web, write as many complimentary, wonderful words as you can.

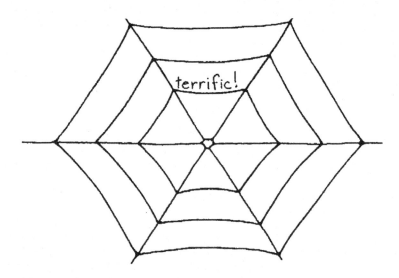

Writing Activity:

Write about a time when you did something wonderful for a friend or a friend did something wonderful for you.

CHARLOTTE'S WEB

CHAPTERS XV – XVIII

Vocabulary: Draw a line from each word on the left to its meaning on the right. Then use the numbered words to fill in the blanks in the paragraph below.

1. resist
2. monotonous
3. enormous
4. confident
5. surpass
6. versatile

a. self-assured
b. be better than
c. able to do many things
d. fight back against
e. always the same; boring
f. very large

. . . .

Wilbur's lonely, _____ ¹ life at the Zuckermans' farm changed once Charlotte came into his life. This _____ ² spider, who could spin and hunt and make clever plans, turned Wilbur into a pig who was happy and _____ .³ Even the Zuckermans could not _____ ⁴ the charm of this pig once they had read "Some Pig" in the web. They were certain that no other pig could _____ ⁵ theirs for beauty and style. Everyone seemed to enjoy Wilbur's _____ ⁶ popularity.

> Read to find out why it is the best of times and the worst of times for Charlotte.

Questions:

1. What was the importance of the cricket's end-of-summer song to Avery and Fern, the young geese, Charlotte, Lurvy, and the maple tree? Do you have similar feelings at the end of summer, or do you look forward to winter? Explain.
2. How did Wilbur try to live up to his reputation?
3. How did the country fair offer a possible dream-come-true for Avery, Lurvy, Mrs. Zuckerman, Mr. Zuckerman, and Wilbur?
4. Why did Charlotte decide to accompany Wilbur to the fair? How did she and the sheep convince Templeton to go along, too?
5. What did Mr. Arable say that made Wilbur faint with fear just when he appeared most radiant?
6. How did Charlotte size up Wilbur's competition?

Chapters XV – XVIII (cont.)

Questions for Discussion:

1. Do you think that most people act according to what is expected of them? How does a good or a bad reputation often become a self-fulfilling prophecy?

2. How do you think Charlotte planned to help Wilbur win?

3. A bittersweet moment is one in which pleasure is mingled with pain. Why might the night at the country fair be considered a bittersweet time?

Literary Device: Foreshadowing

Foreshadowing in literature refers to clues or hints an author gives about what will happen in the story. In the chapters you have just read, what do Charlotte's words and actions seem to foreshadow?

_____

_____

_____

Writing Activity:

Write about a bittersweet time in your own life—one in which pleasure was mingled with pain. Describe what caused you happiness and what caused you to be sad.

CHARLOTTE'S WEB

CHAPTERS XIX – XXII

Vocabulary: Draw a line from each word on the left to its meaning on the right. Then answer the questions about each of the underlined words below.

1. tranquil   a. occurrence that can be observed
2. mimic   b. victory; success
3. phenomenon   c. calm
4. acute   d. beyond what is natural
5. triumph   e. sharp; intense
6. bloated   f. swollen
7. supernatural   g. imitate

. . . .

1. What kind of music makes you feel tranquil?

2. What kinds of animals mimic human behavior?

3. What natural phenomenon can be seen in the sky at night in August?

4. What has ever happened to cause you to feel acute pain?

5. If you ran in a marathon, what would you consider a triumph?

6. What food do you like so much that you could eat it until you were bloated?

7. What book, film, or TV show have you seen that dealt with the supernatural?

> Read to find out what happened at the fair.

Questions:

1. How did Templeton show his insensitivity to Wilbur?
2. What evidence showed that Fern was growing up and losing interest in the barnyard animals?

LEARNING LINKS   15

Chapters XIX – XXII (cont.)

3. When did Charlotte know she saved Wilbur's life?
4. Why was Wilbur awarded a special prize at the fair?
5. How did Charlotte explain why she did so much for Wilbur?
6. What did Wilbur decide to do when it became clear that Charlotte could not return to the barnyard?
7. In what ways did Templeton "come to the rescue" despite his ill-humor?
8. How was Wilbur's homecoming both happy and sad?
9. Even though Charlotte died, why was Wilbur never again friendless and lonely?

Questions for Discussion:
1. What might you conclude about the young spider who said "salutations" upon meeting Wilbur?
2. Why was the word "humble" a perfect description of Wilbur?
3. Why could this book be said to have a happy and a sad ending?
4. In what ways had Charlotte's spider web created webs of friendship and love?

Science Connection:

What scientific facts did you learn about the life cycle of the spider? Why do you think the spider lays so many eggs? What happens to the female after her eggs are laid?

Literary Element: Setting

The setting of a work of literature refers to the time and place in which the story occurs. What was the time span of this story? How many seasons passed? What made you aware of the changing seasons?

Writing Activity:

An obituary is an article written on the occasion of someone's death. Write such an article for Charlotte, describing her talents, her loyalty, and her sacrifice on Wilbur's behalf.

CLOZE ACTIVITY

The following passage is taken from Chapter IV. Read it through completely and then fill in each blank with a word that make sense. Afterwards, you may compare your language with that of the author.

Rain upset Wilbur's plans. Wilbur had planned to go out, this _____,¹ and dig a new hole in his _____.² He had other plans, too. His plans _____³ the day went something like this:

Breakfast _____⁴ six-thirty. Skim milk, crusts, middlings, bits of _____,⁵ wheat cakes with drops of maple syrup _____⁶ to them, potato skins, leftover custard pudding _____⁷ raisins, and bits of Shredded Wheat.

Breakfast _____⁸ be finished at seven.

From seven to _____,⁹ Wilbur planned to have a talk with _____,¹⁰ the rat that lived under his trough. _____¹¹ with Templeton was not the most interesting _____¹² in the world but it was better _____¹³ nothing.

From eight to nine, Wilbur planned _____¹⁴ take a nap outdoors in the sun.

_____¹⁵ nine to eleven he planned to dig _____¹⁶ hole, or trench, and possibly find something _____¹⁷ to eat buried in the dirt.

From _____¹⁸ to twelve he planned to stand still _____¹⁹ watch flies on the boards, watch bees _____²⁰ the clover, and watch swallows in the _____.²¹

Twelve o'clock – lunchtime. Middlings, warm water, apple _____,²² meat gravy, carrot scrapings, meat scraps, stale _____,²³ and the wrapper off a package of _____.²⁴ Lunch would be over at one.

From _____²⁵ to two, Wilbur planned to sleep.

From _____²⁶ to three, he planned to scratch itchy _____²⁷ by rubbing against the fence.

From three _____²⁸ four, he planned to stand perfectly still _____²⁹ think of what it was like to _____³⁰ alive, and to wait for Fern.

At _____³¹ would come supper. Skim milk, provender, leftover _____³² from Lurvy's lunchbox, prune skins, a morsel _____³³ this, a bit of that, fried potatoes, _____³⁴ drippings, a little more of this, a _____³⁵ more of that, a piece of baked _____,³⁶ a scrap of upside-down cake.

Wilbur had gone to sleep thinking about these plans.

POST-READING ACTIVITIES

1. Return to the word web that you began on page twelve of this study guide. Add more complimentary words if you can. Then compare your responses with those of your classmates. Create a new web finding words that best describe Charlotte.

2. **Art Connection:** Design a medal for Wilbur. You may use oaktag or colored construction paper pasted on cardboard. Write a brief statement about him on it. Then glue on a border of colored ribbon or colored paper.

3. Do you like the ending of the book? Would you have preferred another ending? In what ways is this ending true to nature?

4. **Cooperative Learning Activity:** This book is a combination of fact and fantasy. Work with a small cooperative learning group to make a chart listing everything that was true-to-life and scientifically correct and everything that was fantasy. Which list is longer? Compare your lists with those of other groups.

5. Do you think the author wanted you to consider the characters of Charlotte, Wilbur, and Templeton mainly as animals or as humans? What animal-like characteristics did each possess? What human characteristics did each possess?

6. **Pair/Share:** Imagine that you are a television reporter doing a story about the Zuckermans' famous pig for the evening news. Work with a partner to write the script for an interview between yourself [the reporter] and Mr. Zuckerman. Discuss Wilbur's life story, the miracle of the web, and plans for Wilbur's future. Then present your television interview for your class.

7. This is a story about friendship. According to the story, what is the importance of friendship? What qualities should a friend possess? What is life like without a friend? Write a poem about a friend using the following formula:

    Line 1: your friend's name

    Line 2: two things your friend likes to do

    Line 3: three adjectives that describe your friend

    Line 4: your friend's name

8. **Art Connection:** Draw a large circle and divide it into four parts. Label each part with a season of the year. Then write or draw pictures to depict what happened in each season. How does this book show cycles of life?

9. Create a web, such as the one on page three of this study guide for one of your own special friends. Write the person's name in the center of the web and then write descriptive words pertaining to that individual on the lines of the web.

Post-Reading Activities (cont.)

10. **Art Connection:** Create a shoebox diorama depicting one scene from *Charlotte's Web*. Use found objects and simple crafts materials. You might want to show Wilbur in the barn standing under one of Charlotte's special webs.

11. **Story Theatre:** It is fun to read a story with dialogue as though it were a play. Read Chapter Twelve aloud with your classmates taking the following parts:
    - Charlotte
    - Wilbur
    - gander
    - goose
    - goslings
    - sheep
    - lambs
    - Templeton

    One student can read the narration; the characters should read only those words inside the quotation marks. Ignore phrases such as "he said" or "she said." You may want to use simple props so that the animals can be easily identified (e.g. a beak for the goose, a snout for Wilbur, etc.).

12. **Literature Circle:** Have a literature circle discussion in which you tell your personal reactions to *Charlotte's Web*. Here are some questions and sentence starters to help your literature circle begin a discussion.
    - How are you like Fern or Avery? How are you different?
    - How are you like Charlotte?
    - Which character did you like the most? The least?
    - Who else would you suggest read this book?
    - What questions would you like to ask the author about this story?
    - It was funny when...
    - It was sad when...
    - If Wilbur lived at my house...
    - Wilbur learned that...
    - I learned that...

SUGGESTIONS FOR FURTHER READING

* Atwater, Richard, and Florence Atwater. *Mr. Popper's Penguins*. Little, Brown.
* Burnford, Sheila Every. *The Incredible Journey*. Yearling.
* Butterworth, Oliver. *The Enormous Egg*. Little, Brown.
* Cleary, Beverly. *Socks*. HarperCollins.
  _____. *Henry and Beezus*. HarperCollins.
* Dahl, Roald. *Fantastic Mr. Fox*. Puffin.
* Grahame, Kenneth. *The Wind in the Willows*. Dover.
* Howe, James. *Bunnicula*. Great Source.
  _____. *The Celery Stalks at Midnight*. Atheneum.
  King-Smith, Dick. *Ace: The Very Important Pig*. Yearling.
* _____. *Babe: The Gallant Pig*. Yearling.
  Langton, Jane. *The Fledgling*. HarperCollins.
* Lawson, Robert. *Ben and Me*. Little, Brown.
  Milne, A.A. *Winnie the Pooh*. Puffin.
  _____. *The House on Pooh Corner*. Puffin.
  Mowat, Farley. *Owls in the Family*. Yearling.
* Naylor, Phyllis. *Shiloh*. Atheneum.
* O'Brien, Robert. *Mrs. Frisby and the Rats of Nimh*. Aladdin.
* Selden, George. *Cricket in Times Square*. Square Fish.
* Steig, William. *Abel's Island*. Square Fish.
* Van Leeuwen, Jean. *Tales of Oliver Pig*. Square Fish.
* Williams, Margery. *The Velveteen Rabbit*. Grosset & Dunlap.

Other Books by E.B. White

  Second Tree from the Corner. HarperCollins.
* *Stuart Little*. HarperCollins.
* *The Trumpet of the Swan*. HarperCollins.

* NOVEL-TIES Study Guides are available for these titles.

CHARLOTTE'S WEB

ANSWER KEY

Chapters I – III
Vocabulary: 1. runt–smallest animal in a litter 2. injustice–unfairness 3. specimen–example 4. blissful–extremely happy 5. snout–nose 6. vanish–disappear 7. perspiration–sweat 8. commotion–noise and confusion

Questions: 1. Mr. Arable wanted to kill the baby pig because he doubted whether the runt could survive. 2. Fern objected to the killing because she wanted the pig as a pet. 3. Mr. Arable changed his mind because he was sensitive to his daughter's pleas. 4. Fern expressed her contentment because she was completely happy "mothering" the small pig, and the animal was happy, too. 5. Fern's happiness ended when her father told her that he would not support a big pig and that it had to be sold. He was just being practical. 6. Wilbur's new home was a typical well-appointed barn. It was comfortable for the animals, but not as luxurious as Wilbur's former home. 7. The first hint that the animals were communicating with each other occurred when the goose talked to Wilbur. 8. Wilbur ran away because he did not like the barn or the food he was fed. He missed being pampered. Wilbur returned to the farm because he was hungry.

Word Study I: arable–suitable for farming. Answers to the rest of the question will vary.
Word Study II: 1. d 2. f 3. e 4. c 5. a 6. b

Chapters IV – VIII
Vocabulary: 1. h 2. g 3. a 4. c 5. e 6. d 7. f 8. b; 1. anesthetic 2. morsel 3. rigid 4. innocent 5. appalled 6. crafty 7. lair 8. conspiracy

Questions: 1. Wilbur became depressed because he was bored and lonely. 2. The animals were not interested in Wilbur's sadness: the goose was too busy to bother, the lamb would not condescend to play with a pig, and the rat could not understand the idea of "play." 3. Charlotte explained that her hunting and trapping activities were instinctual and necessary for her survival because she was not fed like a barnyard animal. 4. The goose thought that Wilbur was innocent because he didn't know that pigs were usually slaughtered for food when they are grown. 5. Templeton the rat reminded readers of the ugly side of nature because he was a scavenger who appropriated the unhatched goose egg. He would have taken other eggs if they were unguarded. 6. When Wilbur learned from the old sheep that he would be slaughtered, he became hysterical. Charlotte reacted sensibly to the news. She promised to save Wilbur. 7. Mrs. Arable worried about Fern's too vivid imagination when she told her that the animals conversed. Mr. Arable thought it might have happened.

Chapters IX, X
Vocabulary: 1. f 2. h 3. a 4. d 5. b 6. c 7. e 8. g; 1. embarrassed 2. sedentary 3. descend 4. complain 5. twilight 6. gullible 7. vague 8. boastful

Questions: 1. Wilbur's innocence made him think he could help Charlotte spin a web. 2. Charlotte thought humans had inferior web-spinning abilities. 3. Charlotte preferred her own kind of life because it was calm and sedentary as compared to the frantic rush of human activity. 4. Charlotte liked Wilbur's pen because there were lots of flies to catch in her web. 5. Avery teased animals and treated them with some cruelty, while Fern treated them with loving kindness. 6. The smell of the rotten egg deterred Avery from destroying Charlotte's web in the barn.

Chapters XI – XIV
Vocabulary: 1. bewildered–puzzled 2. neglected–disregarded; failed to do 3. destiny–something that is certain to happen 4. incessant–continuous; never ending 5. exertions–vigorous actions 6. radial– arranged like rays 7. orb–formed into a circle 8. solemn–serious 9. tattered–worn and torn

Questions: 1. Charlotte wrote "Some Pig" in her web because she wanted everyone to think that Wilbur was an extraordinary pig who should not be killed. Adults began to think Wilbur was a very special pig. 2. Chapter Eleven got its name because the adults thought the writing in the web was a miracle, rather than the spider's work. The minister and Mr. Zuckerman suggested that the words could be the sign of a miracle. 3. The animals warned that if Wilbur were allowed to die, Templeton would have to forfeit the leftover food he loved in Wilbur's trough. 4. After the appearance of the messages, the Zuckermans had a heightened appreciation of their pig, and Wilbur's own self-esteem improved. 5. Dr. Dorian calmed Mrs. Arable by suggesting that Fern was quite normal, but just more sensitive to the animal world.

CHARLOTTE'S WEB

Chapter XV – XVIII
Vocabulary: 1. d 2. e 3. f 4. a 5. b 6. c; 1. monotonous 2. versatile 3. confident 4. resist 5. surpass 6. enormous
Questions: 1. The end of the summer meant the beginning of school to Avery and Fern, Lurvy knew it was time to dig potatoes, the geese knew their babies were maturing, the maple tree turned red with anxiety, and Charlotte knew she hadn't much time left in the world. Answers to the rest of the questions will vary. 2. To live up to his reputation, Wilbur tried to look radiant by doing back-flips when his audience became bored. 3. Avery dreamed of an adventure on the ferris wheel, Lurvy hoped to win something at a game of skill, Mrs. Zuckerman dreamed of winning a deep freeze unit, Mr. Zuckerman put his hopes on Wilbur—a prize pig. Wilbur knew his life depended upon how well he did at the fair. 4. Charlotte decided to go to the fair because she knew someone needed to write messages about Wilbur. Templeton was convinced to go with promises of the wonderful food he would be able to find. 5. Wilbur became faint from fear when he heard, "You'll get some extra good ham and bacon, Homer, when it comes time to kill that pig." 6. Charlotte thought that Uncle was not as clean as Wilbur and had an unattractive personality. He would, however, be hard to beat because of his size.

Chapters XIX – XXII
Vocabulary: 1. c 2. g 3. a 4. e 5. b 6. f 7. d; Answers to the rest of the vocabulary activity will vary.
Questions: 1. Templeton revealed his insensitivity when he blatantly informed Wilbur that Uncle won a blue ribbon and that probably sealed Wilbur's doom. 2. It was clear that Fern was growing up when she revealed her preference to go out on her own to the midway, rather than stay back with her family at the pig pen. 3. Charlotte knew she had saved Wilbur's life when she learned that Wilbur won a special award. 4. Wilbur was awarded a special prize because of the miracles on the web; people thought he was special, or even blessed. 5. Charlotte explained that her life took on special meaning because she was able to help a friend. 6. When it became clear that Charlotte would not return to the barnyard, Wilbur decided to take Charlotte's egg sac with him, so that he would have the company of her baby spiders when they hatched. 7. Templeton came to the rescue when he found the word possibilities for the web, bit Wilbur's tail to revive him, and got the egg sac for Wilbur. 8. Wilbur's homecoming was happy because he returned a hero, but his homecoming was also sad because he was without his beloved Charlotte. 9. Wilbur was never lonely because he always had the company of Charlotte's descendants.